# Maya the Mouse in the Gluten Free House

First published in Great Britain 2025
Published by HMK Publishing Ltd
Illustration by Anaya


ISBN 978-1-7397209-2-6

This book is for our daughter Maya, who is gluten free and was so brave throughout the long process of being diagnosed with coeliac.

In addition, it is for every other young child, who like Maya, lives a gluten free lifestyle.

One day, Maya the mouse got scared. She was only 6. Her mummy and daddy really cared.

She felt very ill. Her
tummy started to rumble.
Feeling sick, tired and
beginning to grumble.

Maya went to the hospital
to see Doctor Newton.
He told her, "You can no
longer eat Gluten!"

Dental

Mummy and Daddy
knew just what to do.
They asked the shopkeeper Kyle,
'Where is the gluten free aisle?'

SALE

They found lots of
tasty foods to try.
But she had to say 'bye' to
Wheat, Barley and Rye.

Free

Mummy and Daddy taught
Maya to read the food label.
So, she could become
better, well and able.

The teachers at school
put things in place.
Providing healthy dinners,
with no gluten trace.

Maya had to stop eating
bread, pasta, pizza and pie.
Then told all of her friends,
the reason why.

We all need to help
Maya follow the code.
To guide her along the
gluten free road.

Now Maya lives in a
gluten free house.
She's a happy and healthy,
sweet little mouse.

Printed in Great Britain
by Amazon

61364193R00016